The Adventures of
Belle and Nick
The Rescue Ponies

The Adventures of
Belle and Nick
The Rescue Ponies

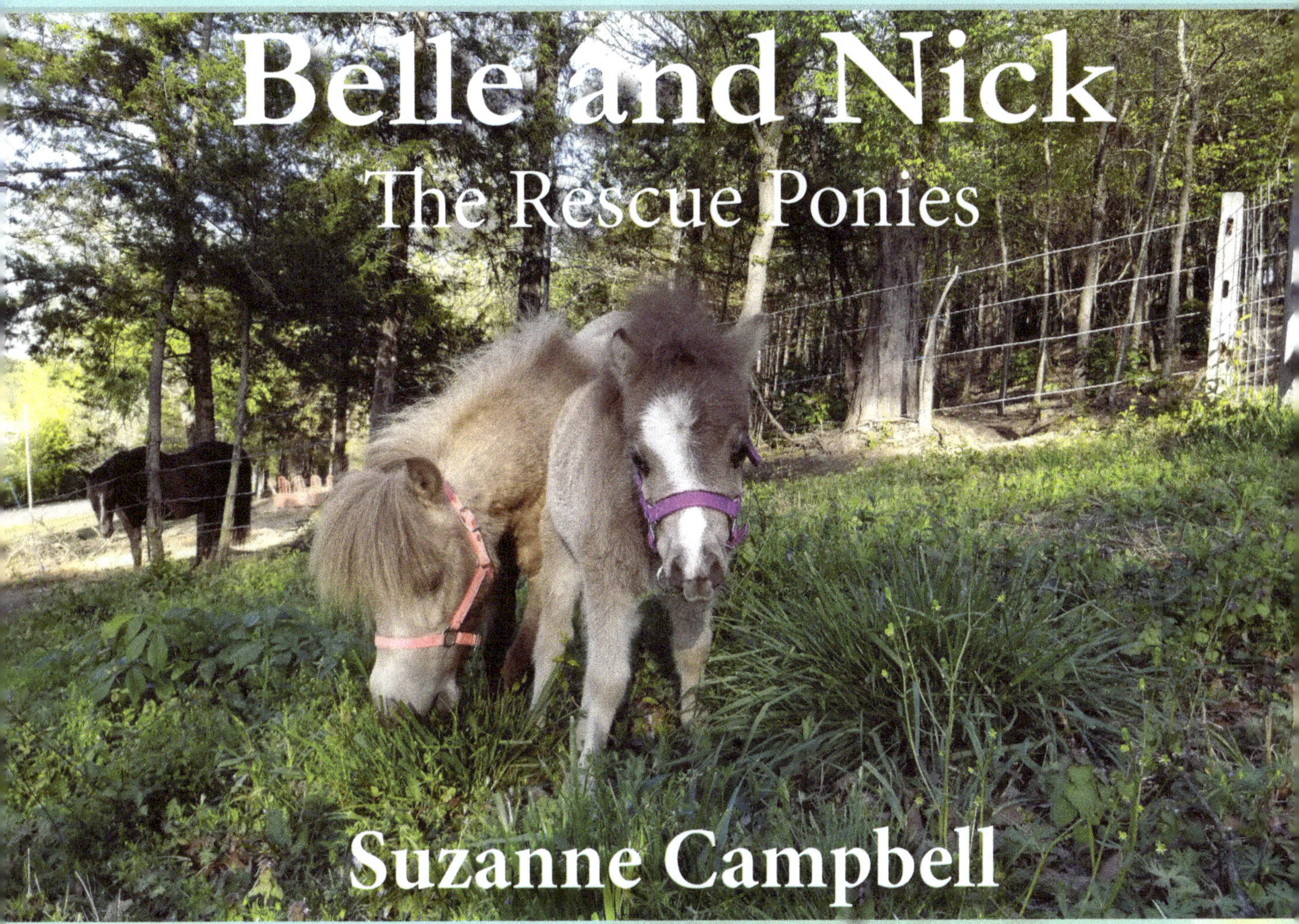

Suzanne Campbell

TONTI
PRESS

Published by Tonti Press Little Rock, Arkansas
Copyright © 2019 by Suzanne Campbell. All rights reserved.

All art created by Suzanne Campbell

First published August 2019

Manufactured in the United States of America

ISBN-13: 978-0-9998734-4-1

Library of Congress Control Number:2019910008

Notice: The information in this book is true and complete to the best of our knowledge. It is offered without guarantee on the part of the author. The author disclaims all liability in connection with the use of this book.

All rights reserved. No part of this book may be reproduced or transmitted in any form whatsoever without prior written permission from the author or publisher, except in the case of brief quotations embodied in critical articles and reviews.

A portion of the proceeds from this book goes to local animal rescue efforts.

I dedicate this book in memory of my mother, who always told me you can judge a person's true character by the way they treat animals.

It was a cool, bleak morning in late October in Arkansas.

The farmer's wife waited for the horse trailer to arrive, loaded with horses and donkeys traveling to their new forever homes.

On board, tucked into a corner, was the smallest horse she had ever seen, here to start her new life at Three Sisters Farm.

The farmer's wife spoke in hushed tones, as she led her from the trailer, all the while thinking to herself,

"What a pretty little thing she is with her long mane and tail.

I think I will name her Belle."

The next day Belle settled in to her new surroundings.

The vet had been called, just to make sure she was healthy, even though she was quarantined from the other horses on the farm.

As time went by, Belle made friends with
Mocha the donkey,
Moonpie the mini,
Rad the old Morgan mare,
and Rhen the Haflinger pony.

All was happy on the farm.

One day the farmer's wife noticed that Belle was getting rather plump, and was concerned she had been eating too much.

But she also thought,
what if she is going to have a baby?

The vet was called yet again.

Would you believe it, she was going to have a baby very soon!

A flurry of activity started on the farm.

A special pen with a shelter was built, and the farmer's wife made sure Belle was kept in the barn at night.

Early one morning, the farmer's wife went to do her barn chores as usual. She said

"Good Morning Belle. How are you today?"

To her amazement, standing beside her was a small fluffy grey foal.

"Oh my goodness!" she exclaimed, "He is so tiny!"

The little pony was smaller than the farmer's dog.

It wasn't long before Belle and Nick ventured out of the barn to explore.

At first he stuck to his mother's side like glue.

As the weeks passed,
he got braver.

Belle would be frantic with her whinnies, calling to him to come back.

He would scamper back.

As he grew his coat changed to a light chocolate brown.

It wasn't long until Nick was taller than his mother.

Little Nick loves to play with all of his newfound friends,

especially Smudge, the farm dog, who is about his size.

On the weekends, there would be
more adventure,
as the farmer's wife's grandchildren would come to
help with barn chores.

They would brush and comb his long tail,

and fuss over him,
and feed him tiny horse pellets.

Nick would love to gallop up the steep hills
as fast as his legs could carry him,
to see all there was to see
at Three Sisters Farm.

Then in an instant
something would startle him,
and he would go off
galloping and bucking
back to the safety of his
mother Belle.

As the sun sets between the trees on Three Sister Farm, all the animals are settling down to rest,

whilst Nick is dreaming of the next day's great adventure with his friends tomorrow.

BELLE AND NICK'S FAVORITE SUMMER TREAT

4 cups of miniature horse feed
1 cup alfalfa pellets
3 carrots, chopped
2 cups apples, chopped
4 cups watermelon, chopped

Mix and serve one cup per mini.

Don't forget to give the big horses a chunk of watermelon, too!

The author with Nick, Belle and her grandchildren.

Suzanne Campbell is a lifelong Certified Executive Chef with the ACF Culinary Federation. She has won numerous awards during her culinary career, most recently Chef Educator of the Year as a culinary instructor with the University of Arkansas Pulaski Technical College Culinary Arts and Hospitality Management Institute.

Born in Scotland, Campbell grew up in a pub in the Lake District. Her happiest memories are of her galloping horses across the beach and learning cooking skills from her grandmother.

In her retirement, she has learned another art she can share with her five grandchildren, teaching them the responsibility of working and looking after the animals on her Central Arkansas farm.

Mrs. Campbell still rides and drives in competitive horse shows with her horses and ponies.

www.ingramcontent.com/pod-product-compliance
Lightning Source LLC
Chambersburg PA
CBHW061148010526
44118CB00026B/2908